AF593955

Peynet
LOVE, SWEET LOVE

SOUVENIR PRESS

First British Edition published 1986 by Souvenir Press Ltd,
43 Great Russell Street, London WC1B 3PA
and simultaneously in Canada

ISBN 0 285 62778 3

Printed in Great Britain by
Richard Clay (The Chaucer Press) Ltd,
Bungay, Suffolk

Heart to heart

And the family

But how could there be anyone else?

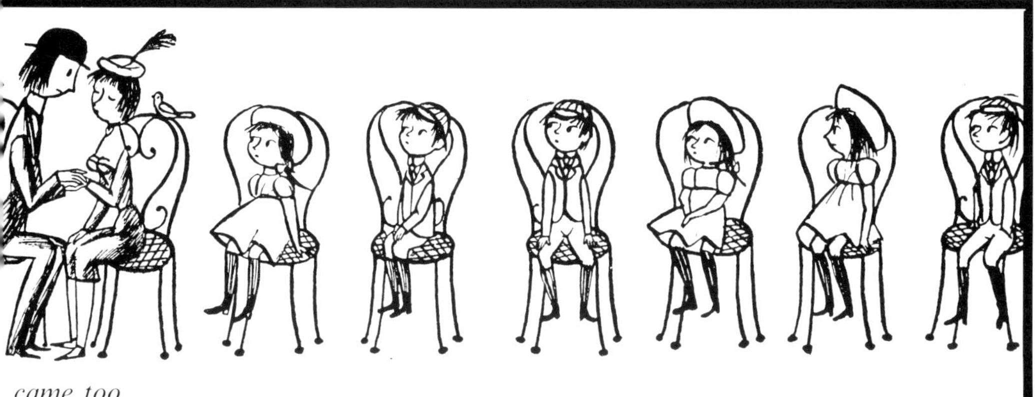

came too . . .

She loves me . . . I think . . .

See if I care!

All we need is love

Do you feel a little warmer now?

You're too late! They got there first

I've got enough to keep us in clover . . .

I'd never have married you if I'd known we'd be living rough

Of course I don't mind hanging on, but do get a move on

Have you ever seen the moon as close as this?

Look at those dreamers up there. It's the same every night

I hope I haven't kept you waiting too long

Three and a half hours late! Where can she have got to?

The best ones aren't on display. Come and have a look inside

You guessed right the first time

1

2

LOVERS OF THE
WORLD UNITE

3

4

The Lover's Party

She likes me . . . she loves me . . . she's besotted with me . . .

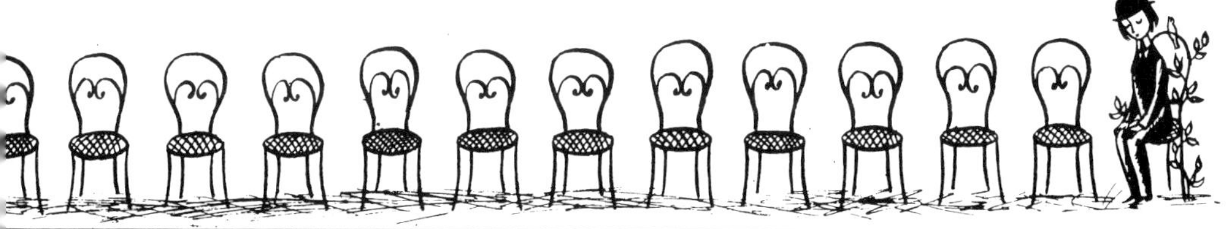

Take no notice, mummy's a bit strait-laced

I've been dreaming about you all night . . .

Can't you imagine it? With geraniums in the windows and a little cat on the roof?

Oh, look! Shooting stars! Make a wish, darling!

'Such stuff as dreams are made on . . .'

It's only my hands that need warming up . . .

Yng mn, gd-lkng, affectionate, seeks attractive, loving yng wmn, with view to marriage. Bad housekeepers need not apply

Wake up, can't you! I need the eiderdown to warm my feet

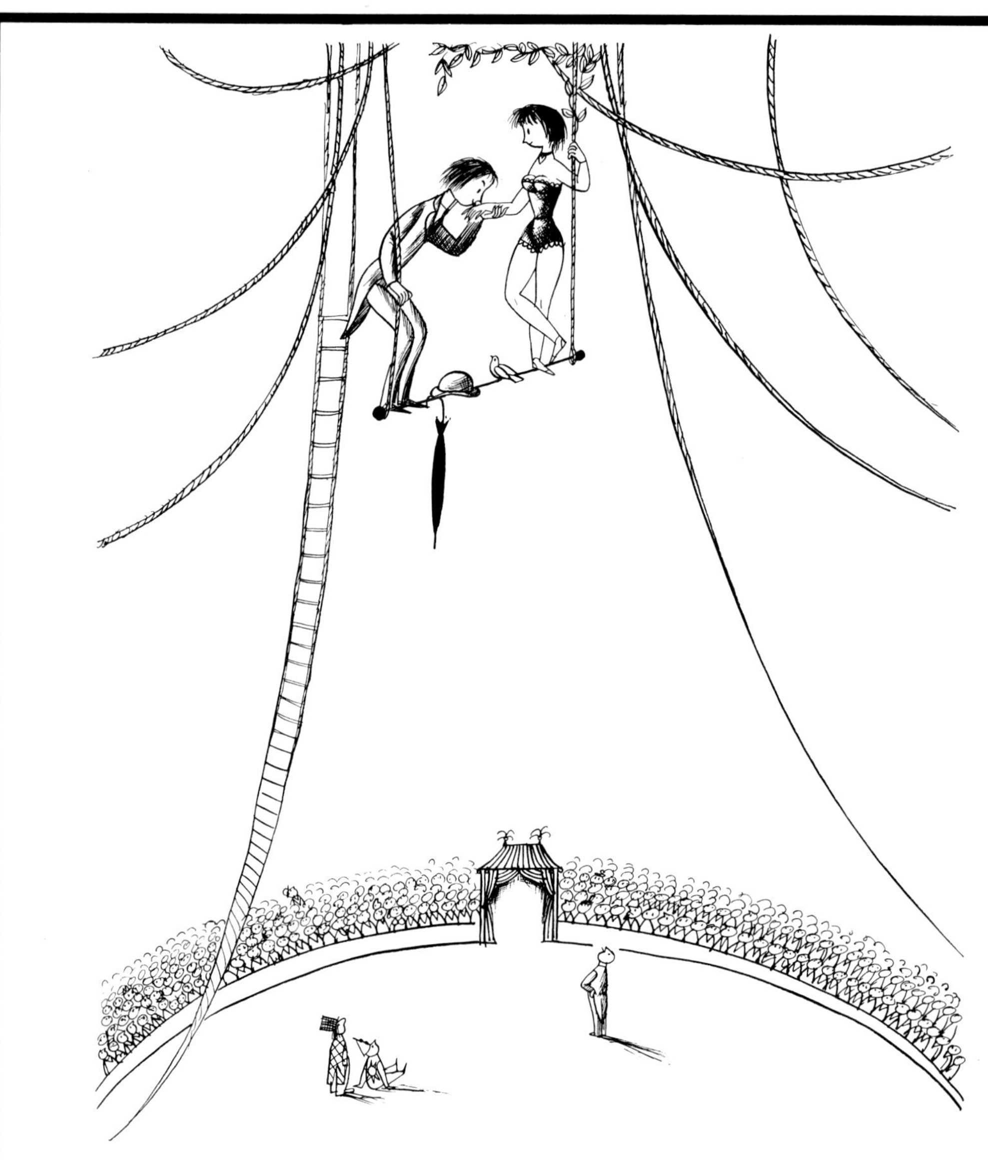

But you said I should come up and see you some time

Oh, come on, let's forget romance for a few minutes and get down to business

She loves me, she loves me not, loves me, loves me not, love-not-love-not-love . . .

Singing in the rain . . .

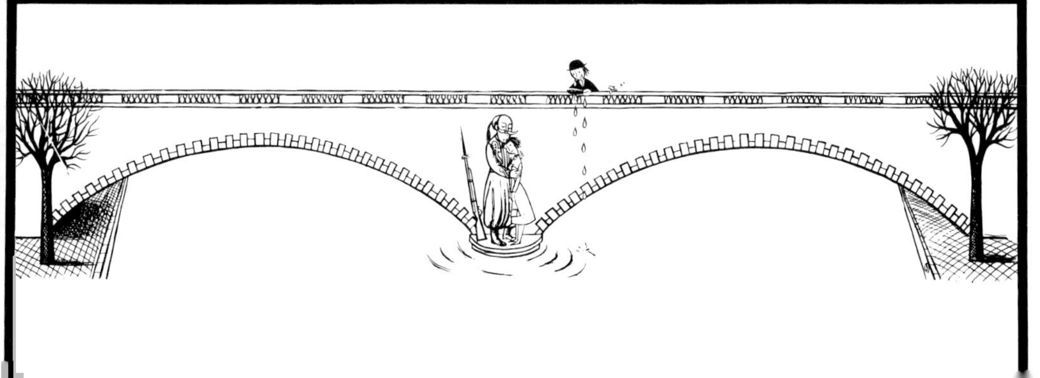

How stupid, to let a silly quarrel come between us

That's the end of that honeymoon

I'm not free tonight, but I'll leave these with you instead

1
2
3
4

Could I trouble you to hang your washing elsewhere?

I bet you can't write a love song with just two notes

Bird's nest soup coming up!

THE END